Peas in a Pod
Finger Rhymes

Chosen by Kate Ruttle and Richard Brown
Illustrated by Adriano Gon

CAMBRIDGE
UNIVERSITY PRESS

The Beehive

Here is the beehive.

Where are the bees?

Hidden away where nobody sees.

2

Here they come creeping out of the hive,

one,

two,

three,

four,

five.

BZZZZZZ

HONEY

Sowing Seeds

Four seeds in a hole,
four seeds in a hole.

One for the mouse,

one for the crow,

one to rot,

and one to grow.

How Do They Grow?

Flowers grow like this.

Trees grow like this.

But I grow like this!

Granny's Apple Tree

On my granny's apple tree,

five red apples I can see.

Some for you and some for me.

Let's pick some apples from the tree.

Cherries for Tea

Once I found a cherry stone.
I put it in the ground,

and when I came to look at it,
a tiny shoot I found.

The shoot grew up and up each day
and soon became a tree.

I picked the rosy cherries then
and ate them for my tea.

Peas in a Pod

Five fat peas in a pea pod pressed.

 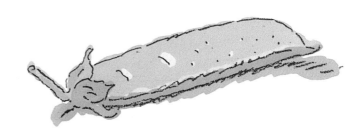

One grew, two grew,

and so did all the rest.

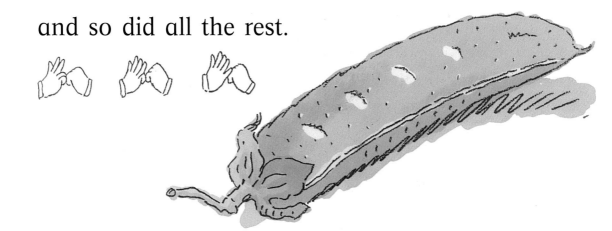

They grew and they grew
and they did not stop,

until, one day, the pod went . . .